JAMAICIZMS
Illustrations And Annotations
Written By: Fay Akyaah Gyapong

Illustrations By: Visoeale

An homage to my dear mother affectionately known as "Nen" or "Nena" and my dear Aunt Sybil who is depicted on the cover. The proverbs are trying to reflect a Jamaican dialect known as *Patòis*.

Proverb:

One finga kyant ketch lice.

Meaning: Teamwork and cooperation is needed to achieve goals for the common good.

Proverb:

Mooma hear deh a hilltop.

Meaning: A mother can pick out her child's cry from afar.

Proverb:

Once a man twice a child.

Meaning: When a person reaches very old age, his or her mental or physical capacity is often reduced to that of a child.

Proverb:
Me come fa drink milk, me nah come fa count cow.

Meaning: Not here to gossip.

Proverb:

Who feels it knows it.

Meaning: The one who experiences something difficult or challenging has more understanding and empathy than someone who has not experienced it.

Proverb:
Stranger dunno back door.

Meaning: Some people think they know who you are, when really they don't.

Proverb:

Cast your bread upon wahta and it comes back to you.

Meaning: Do good things and good things happen to you.

Proverb:

Dry eyed person.

Meaning: An envious person.

Proverb:

Long rope short ketch.

Meaning: Eventually one's bad deeds catches up with one.

Proverb:

Not same day leaf drop it rotten.

Meaning: The consequences of a mistake may not be felt for years, but will eventually have an impact.

Proverb:

Bend a tree when it is young.

Meaning: It is easier to train a child with good habits and behaviors when they are young.

Proverb:

Same knife that stick sheep stick goat.

Meaning: A person who says or does something malevolent to one person will likely treat you the same way.

Proverb:

Take sleep and mark death.

Meaning: Some things are not what they appear to be, so do your due diligence.

JAMAICIZMS
Illustrations And Annotations

Written By: Fay Akyaah Gyapong

Illustrations By: Visoeale

ISBN: 978-1-66789-028-9